IN THE SHADOW OF TWO THEME PARK CASTLES

HAUNTED ORLANDO

Stories Told by Ting Rappa of American Ghost Adventures

Written By Debra Walloch Hoffman

INTRODUCTION:

Most people have some thoughts one way or
the other about the existence of spirits or an
afterlife. For many of us these beliefs are both
born and cultivated by our background or
culture, while then perhaps becoming
transformed and cemented by our personal
experiences. As a Vietnamese émigré at less
than two years of age, my family and I brought
with us our Asian values. We were taught from
birth that followers of Buddhism worshipped
the dead, but were, under no circumstances, to
speak or interact with these spirits. Yet, as
assimilation into American life took root and
our family expanded, my siblings and I would be
exposed to, and then sometimes embraced,
different religious faiths. Some of these new
belief systems offered a completely different
view of the spiritual world altogether.
Personally, the exposure to these new concepts

served to convince me that there is a greater being beyond myself and the physical world. With a touch of rebelliousness, I was determined more than ever to explore this world despite all the parental warnings and prohibitions. It may have also helped that every rental property my parents owned was found to be haunted, or that our family name actually means "house of spirits"!

The creation of American Ghost Adventures (AGA) paranormal tour and investigation group in 2010 was the inevitable culmination of this lifelong passion, and after I had joined another local ghost tour group in 2004, as a shareholder/marketing person. Raised in Orlando, I already knew that there were more stories to be told and fun to be had, outside of the glittering fantasy and magical thrills of the theme parks just down the road. With each investigation in and around the city that had its beginnings as a frontier outpost, our group has interacted with the fascinating spirits of those who have gone before us, and either continue to linger or stop by to visit. It might surprise most visitors to learn that Orlando has a colorful history, with more to offer than jaw-dropping rides and suntans in January. Whether one wants to get away from everyday life to experience the happiest place, or the darkest place, we offer one alternative. To date, we've welcomed a multitude of guests from all over the world to experience a different, darker kind of thrill on our tours, in locations they may never have heard of before, but surely will never forget!

The stories in this book are actual personal experiences of mine and other AGA team members, or when specifically noted, legends and stories told to us by others who have experiences in the mentioned locales. In some cases, names or other identifying information have been changed to protect the privacy of individuals or locations. In doing our investigations and tours, we have selected known haunted locations and have either been invited by the owners or management to investigate, or we have obtained permission to do so. Many places embrace their haunted designation and allow public access, while others do not. Ghost hunters must always obey the laws and respect the rules and privacy of the living! This makes it easier for all of us to access sites, whether as an industry professional or an amateur. As a tour company, we only take our guests into places where we feel safe and comfortable, and where we have experienced spirits who wish to interact with us. Because we visit some locations on a daily basis, each tour or investigation is uniquely different, often adding to the known history of a place, as we document each and every paranormal interaction. In many cases, our guests even come away with stories of their own, and maybe a few very interesting pictures!

While enjoying this book, please know that it is not my intention, nor that of AGA, to either prove the existence of ghosts, or convince the skeptics to change their belief systems. The real purpose of both the stories and our tours is to entertain, offer some interesting history, and if possible, introduce others to our experiences and some of our other worldly, "high spirited" friends! We always ask our guests to keep an open mind and enjoy themselves, as well as to indulge their imaginations, and I would ask my readers to do the same. It is for each individual to decide how they would describe their own experience. For all of the believers, hopefully the stories and experiences will be added to their own paranormal collection. Whatever the scenario, after reading this book, one might just want to wonder whenever they find themselves alone... "Am I really alone?"

Ting Rappa

American Ghost Adventures

Ting Rappa Founder of

American Ghost Adventures

UP CLOSE AND PERSONAL

The Lady in the Bathtub

Every believer in ghosts has that one moment somewhere during their lifetime that is deeply etched in memory. It is the one that marks the turning point between normal life and something else entirely. I am no different. Although spirits have been a part of my life since I can remember, it was a particular childhood experience that made me first take notice.

Tucked within the tree- lined Orlando neighborhoods, I remember very clearly the house my parents owned on Livingston Street in the early 1980's when I was about ten. It was one of numerous rental properties they were to own in the city, and I often accompanied them to the homes when they were in need of cleaning between tenants. The first time I set foot in this house it felt "odd". Moreover, I could not understand why I was inexplicably drawn to the bathroom, and could not tolerate being alone in the back bedroom as it made me nervous. I simply did not like the house.

One day, I announced to my mother that the lady who once owned the house had died in the bathtub and she was still there. My mother gave me a sharp look and angrily demanded to know why I would say such a thing. I couldn't explain how I knew. I just did. I was told to forget that notion and it was not mentioned again. And in the Asian tradition, she nevertheless burned incense to bless the house with good luck. Despite the lack of parental acknowledgement, I lost much of my fear anyway in sensing that the old lady was actually protective of the home and approved of us as the new owners.

But it would be decades before I would learn the truth from my mother. It would not be until around 2010 when I asked about the Livingston Street home, which she had sold some years previously, that I would find out a closely guarded family secret. My mother could actually see and feel spirits!

She told me that around 2004, she put the house up for sale. Although many buyers came to see the property, they would all walk away, citing its "odd" feeling. Finally, one day my mother went to the house alone and pleaded with the old lady's spirit. She confided that she herself was getting old and could not take care of the property any longer, while asking if maybe the spirit could just back off a little so she could sell the house. And miracle of miracles, the very next couple to come see the house bought it! After that, my mother never heard of any paranormal activity from the new owners, which makes me wonder whether the old lady just moved on, or did she continue to follow my mother?

Through the years I would learn that other rental properties that my parents owned were also haunted by overhearing the various tenants relate their experiences to my parents. It should be noted that in Florida, there is no legal real estate requirement to disclose that a building or home may be considered "haunted", and thus my parents never received any warnings from previous owners. And just as my mother had the ability to see spirits, my father would confess shortly before he passed away that he could see them as well. With this admission that he saw them but ignored them, he also proffered a warning. Knowing that I could see them too, he cautioned me never to "play" with the spirits, as some were evil. As an example, he told me that whenever he saw a particular little girl, trouble always ensued.

As everyone may well have guessed by reading this book, I have yet to stop "playing" with them.

Housemate from Hell

As I grew older I had fewer ghostly experiences, and more often than not, when they did happen my parents would not talk about it, or we would find some other explanation for an occurrence. Incense would be burned and life would go on. It was not until I was a young adult that I had my first "live-in" ghost.

The house was old, dated, and more to the point, rough and in no way charming. Its one saving grace was a huge oak tree outside the large living room picture window. But the rent was cheap enough, perfect for two young couples embarking on their independence. So with my then boyfriend and two other friends, we moved in, settling into our room facing the street, with a view of the old oak tree.

 Almost immediately, I noticed the "off" feeling of the house, but chalked it up to being in a strange new place. As time went on, however, it became difficult not to notice "things". When in the bathroom showering, there was an overwhelming sense of being watched, and I would always hurry and get out of there as quickly as humanly possible. Darting shadows and unexplainable cold spots were also tough to ignore by virtually everyone in the house.

One day, during a heated argument, my boyfriend stormed into the bathroom with me tailing close behind him. A cigarette dangling from his mouth, he proceeded to angrily strike matches, all of which fizzled out immediately and were tossed into the shower stall. While pausing to stare at each other in the mirror, we watched in horror as the matches in the shower behind us began to light all on their own! After running from the room screaming to alert the rest of our housemates, we all re- entered the bathroom to find that the matches had again extinguished.

My boyfriend was in a panic, muttering, "Oh my gosh, it's starting again." It was then I learned that he had endured a childhood full of eerie paranormal experiences of which he was not eager to repeat. From seeing spirits, to a ring that when thrown away would mysteriously reappear, to the ceiling opening up, the litany went on. At first I was skeptical and thought this was part of some elaborate prank that he and the others were trying to pull on me.

The events that would follow proved it was no prank. One day, while we were all standing in the kitchen, I noticed a puddle of liquid on the terrazzo floor. I immediately demanded that whoever had caused the spill needed to clean it up ASAP. As I emphatically pointed to the offending puddle, we all watched incredulously as it disappeared right before our eyes! "What puddle?" one of us managed to stammer, although for the life of me, I can't remember who in that moment. An investigation of the plumbing and appliances in the immediate area yielded no reasonable explanation.

Later that same night, everyone in the household was awakened by the sounds of loud footsteps on the ceiling. Terrified, the two men headed out the front door with a baseball bat to confront the trespasser on the roof. They found nobody outside, but almost at once, the leaves on the lawn seemed to "scurry" as if unseen feet were running through them! Now we were all thinking it. We have a ghost!

After that, the unease throughout the house only seemed to increase. When the story is Hollywood scripted and projecting from a screen, the terrifying chills are delicious. In real life, not so much. The final straw came when I returned from my college class one afternoon to be greeted by a neighbor. The gentleman wanted to know what we were doing with an axe in the house, as he saw a shadow pacing back in forth in front of the window carrying an axe. My slack jaw and bugged eyes probably gave it all away. I had been the last to leave and the first to come home that day. There was nobody else inside! The neighbor casually added that most of the renters never stayed more than six months, if that, and he'd wondered why. He even bravely went inside the house to see if anybody was there. Of course, there was nobody. That night my boyfriend and I made our beds in my car outside, and our friends, likewise stayed elsewhere, with none of us ever to sleep there again.

We officially lasted at that address for only three months. Even after one of my housemates brought in a priest to bless the house, I could not stay there after that and sought refuge at a friend's, before finding a new place to rent. Axe-wielding shadow people are truly the stuff of nightmares. The place so frightened me, it would be ten years before I could even drive down that street again!

His Name Was Peter

It was during a brief time living in Tampa, before returning to Orlando and what would be my calling, that I would learn some very interesting and important things about ghosts and hauntings. For that reason, I will begin this story there.

Now married and the stay at home mother of a nine month old son, I was excited to begin an adventure in which just the three of us would share our first official home together. Our apartment community, situated near Waters and Dale Mabry Avenues featured cozy units, four to a building, and we eagerly settled in to one on the first floor near the laundry room. My husband worked long hours, while our son and I shared the days together. Life was running smoothly. But that wouldn't last very long.

With the last house experience still very fresh in mind, I couldn't help but notice the strange occurrences as they began. The television would come on by itself, or mysteriously change channels to cartoon shows. Toys would play all on their own, and different household objects would be moved from one place to another, none of which could be attributed to an absent husband, or a nine month old baby. And then there was that feeling of being watched again.

During hysterical daytime calls to my husband I would beg him to come home. At first we both wondered if this could be the same spirit from the earlier house.

One afternoon after the television went crazy on its own and I was frightened out of my wits, I grabbed the baby and went outside. My neighbor, having returned from picking up her own children from school, saw that I was noticeably shaken and asked whether I was all right. When I told her that I believed my house was haunted, she calmly responded, "Yes it is." I thought the ground would come up to hit me square in the face!

She invited me upstairs, where her three year-old and seven year-old excitedly shouted, "You got to meet Peter!" Peter, as it turns out, was a nine or ten year- old boy who had died in a house fire, and whose spirit followed them from their last apartment to this one, because he felt like a part of the family.

The children talked to him and played with him as if he were any ordinary living boy. It seemed that he had visited our apartment as well because we had new and different toys. They told me not to be afraid, and assured that Peter was friendly, but I felt little comfort at the time. Upon returning downstairs to our apartment, I spoke out loud to Peter, asking him not to scare me or show himself to me. And for the time he was with us, I never saw him.

Not too long afterward, life changed in a major way, and my husband and I divorced. I promptly moved back to Orlando with my son, settled back in with my parents, and began working two jobs. It was then that I would learn firsthand that ghosts can indeed follow people and travel from place to place. For one thing, I could still sense Peter around me, just as I had in Tampa.

On a morning when exhaustion had defeated me and I'd decided to sleep in a bit, I felt a violent shake that snapped me awake.

My son, who had grown quite adept at climbing out of his crib, was in the process of scaling the tall dresser in the room. The dresser, laden with glass collectibles and knick-knacks, was just about to tip over, as I sprung out of bed to catch it. But not before all the glass slid off the top and shattered on the floor, sending pieces in every direction. Miraculously, neither I nor my son was hit by even one little shard. I knew then that it was Peter who had awakened me and protected both of us.

A few months later we moved into an Orlando apartment with some roommates, and before long, they too were witnessing paranormal events. No longer afraid of our little companion, I would tell them that it was just Peter, and that he was a harmless protector. In no time at all, he would playfully entertain us and our friends, turning on toys and stopping them as soon as somebody approached.

One day, my roommate and her boyfriend got into one of their usual arguments, and he decided he would record her to show her how she sounded. He opened a package with a brand new cassette tape, the technology of the time, and put into the tape recorder. As they argued, everybody else wisely cleared out of the room. Later that evening he summoned me and told me that I really needed to listen to the tape, which I was reluctant to do. But when he played it, it became clear why he was so excited. With their arguing audible in the background, the innocent voice of a young boy is heard near the microphone, "Helloooooo my name is Peeeeeter." There were no little boys present in the apartment at that time!

And that was my first experience with electronic voice phenomenon, or EVP, where a voice is recorded that was not audible to the human ear.

I still get chills when I relive that moment, and it made me eager to further explore the possibility of these spirit communications. It also validated the paranormal experiences that we were all having. Eventually, I got my life back on track, and Peter went on his way. I would like to think that he's gone off to protect some other family, in the same way as he had for us, our very own little guardian angel!

In my new job for a marketing company, I came into contact with many hotel concierges in the Orlando area. Around Halloween one year, during conversations about local attractions and my own personal paranormal experiences, one concierge revealed that he also worked for a downtown ghost tour company, and invited me on a tour. Upon doing so, I was amazed to find out how many "normal" businesses and restaurants, some of which I had frequented before, were haunted. Learning the history and being able to actually go inside and investigate

these places just made me want to know more.
And thus, a ghost tour career was born!

THE PHENOMENAL CITY

Emily and Friends

Before 1908, and the time that Orlando became known as "The City Beautiful", it was "The Phenomenal City".

Nobody knows why a contest was called to change the nickname, or why it stopped being phenomenal, but rest assured, phenomena abound here! Many of its oldest downtown buildings and newer construction alike are haunted, whether or not the living that work or reside there will admit it.

From a cow town in the 1840's to a burgeoning citrus industry center, settlers from northern states and "across the pond" poured into the area to stake their homestead claims. The arrival of the railroad in 1880 helped the city grow and thrive, and soon businesses rose up around it. Even after a devastating citrus freeze in 1894 drove some back to their origins, many hearty souls prevailed. The boom years of the early 1920's further defined the Orlando skyline, as commerce continued to take root, and sturdier buildings proudly exhibited newly distinguished facades.

One such building is the home of the Orange County Regional History Center at 65 E. Central Boulevard. Built in 1927 to serve as the fifth courthouse in Orlando, the site played a role in some of the most infamous national events of the twentieth century. Notorious serial killer Ted Bundy was tried and convicted there in 1980. But it was the courthouse shootings in 1984 that killed one bailiff and critically injured another one, along with a Corrections officer, which would spark the courthouse security measures practiced across the country today.

It would be as a new member of a downtown ghost tour team that I had an opportunity to experience firsthand the spirits who also frequent this venue, and to hone my skills at positively attracting and interacting with them. As the final stop on our tours at the time, we were able to conduct after hours paranormal research investigations, with only our tour group, a security guard and several cleaning personnel present in the building.

Or should I say, these were the only living ones who would be present!

With nearly daily visits, in time we were able to identify various spirits and even become familiar with their habits, likes and dislikes. Undoubtedly the most talked about ghost at the history center has to be Emily. A friendly and seemingly happy girl of seven or eight, she is seen, heard and felt by many visitors. Whether peeking down the staircase, running down the hall giggling, or playing with guests' clothing and jewelry, she is a delight to all who encounter her. Sadly, her backstory is much less than warm and fuzzy.

As the story goes, Emily reportedly returns to the former courthouse in search of her family, in the place where she had last seen them in life. Allegedly the victim of abuse by her father, and with a mother who was unfit to care for her, she became a ward of the state.

While in state care she subsequently contracted, and then died of, pneumonia, never having had a chance to reunite with her family. Even though she has been told that her parents are no longer there, Emily still chooses to return.

Knowing that she favors women with jewelry, and generally loves shiny objects, I was soon able to determine right off the bat which of my tour guests would intrigue her to come to the table at which they were seated. She was instinctively drawn to the ladies who were mothers, and especially those who had snacks in their purses. So, how do I know this?

In paranormal investigation, or ghost hunting if you will, one of the basic tools is the EMF detector, or K2 meter, which is also utilized by electricians to locate electrical leaks and emissions. With the theory being that spirits are made up of energy, they can also be picked up by this instrument, once all other possible electrical sources are eliminated.

When energy is detected, a series of colored lights will light up from green to orange, all the way up to red, depending on the strength. Spirits can manipulate these lights to intelligently respond to our questions, and even favor certain individuals by lighting up only their meters. As many of our tour guests who were armed with meters could attest, Emily was quite good at it!

During the summer months, the history center offered day camp sessions for children, many of whom Emily would "play" with, along with their toys. It was while we had a woman psychic on tour that we learned that Emily longed for her own toy too. So we bought her a small, pocket-sized teddy bear, which became a "trigger object" to entice her to interact with us. She loved the bear, and we never showed up at the center without it. Or at least we didn't until one particular, remiss guide accidentally took the bear home in her pocket for an entire week, only failing to return with it because there were no tours during that time.

Bad luck is as much a part of an individual's belief system as, well ghosts, and can't always be explained as caused by any one event or action. But I might beg to differ here. This guide was plagued by one miserable occurrence after another. From her car having mysterious mechanical problems, to her phone intermittently failing, among other misfortunes, she had one of her worst weeks ever. But it would take an out of town investigative trip to Clearwater, Florida, to put Emily, and even our whole view of spirits in perspective.

During this away investigation, a psychic, who was also present with our group, informed us that a girl named "Emily" had followed us to the location. Well that sounded very interesting. As the psychic was an old school friend of mine, I knew him personally and knew that I could trust him to be honest.

He went on to say that, although he normally doesn't do it, she was begging to communicate with us physically through him. He asked that I make sure that he didn't injure himself, before talking to thin air, and stating, "Okay, but only this one time!" I wasn't sure what he meant until we all experienced what happened next.

The psychic's facial features started to transform, and he began to speak in a voice that wasn't even close to his own. It was a high pitched little girl's voice! He quickly turned to one of our stunned guides and asked him, "Why don't you ever bring the frosted animal crackers anymore?" He then immediately pivoted and sternly addressed the "teddy bear-poaching" guide with, "I had to teach you a lesson. It's my toy!" The interaction abruptly stopped, after about thirty to forty-five seconds, before any of us could even gather ourselves to react.

Even more incredible, the psychic wanted to know what Emily had to say, not having any idea what just transpired.

He also was completely unaware beforehand that the one guide brought animal crackers to the history center, and that one had mistakenly taken the teddy bear home with her. As he was feeling slightly dizzy from the encounter, we had to sit him down. But it was a total WOW moment! Before that experience, I probably wouldn't have believed the story myself. In fact, the experience was so powerful for my psychic friend, that it propelled him into a life of Christian ministry that continues to this day.

I personally got to know Emily quite well over all the years that we did tours at the history center. In the beginning, she would even try to follow me home. One night, as I got into my van, my infant son's toys began going off all by themselves, and his musical mobile started to play. One might suggest that the shaking of the vehicle, or some motion sensory effect, could have set them off. But then one might be wrong.

I turned and said to the vacant back seat, "Emily, you can't go home with me sweetie. I will visit you again soon, please go back inside." The mobile immediately stopped playing.

On another occasion, I was replenishing equipment at the history center and brought my fourteen month old son along with me. While seated on the stairs talking to another guide, my son facing me on my lap, he suddenly stopped twirling my hair and sucking his thumb, and shouted at the empty space beside us, "My mommy!" A not very sociable child at the time, who spoke few words, he began humming and swatting at the air next to us, as if to ward of something, or somebody. And suddenly I knew what to say, "Emily, he's just a baby. He doesn't know any better. It's okay."

Emily is not alone at the history center, and the staff has many stories of other paranormal encounters. One spirit is believed to be that of a bailiff, whose presence is denoted by a disembodied male voice which asks, "Can I help you?" They also report that when first entering the building in the morning, the sound of a whole bunch of people can be heard whispering and chatting in the courtroom, although of course, nobody is there.

Other occurrences include an apparition holding a bathroom stall door in the first floor women's restroom. In the Grand Jury Room, many have felt a presence there that primarily affects men, making them feel nauseous whenever they reach a particular spot in the room. Yet another spirit paces in front of the Grand Jury Room. Legend has it that he was a jury member who died before he got a chance to cast his vote during a trial, causing him to pace for eternity.

Anyone now have a verdict on the history center? One might suggest, "Haunted as charged"!

One of the trigger objects we use on our investigation and a K2 meter to help us detect and find energy.

The Power of 12

Sometimes an event happens that so profoundly effects us , that it makes us ask questions about life itself. And perhaps more reluctantly, the afterlife.

Although I have had numerous such instances in my own lifetime, this is one that is well worth relating.

In the fall of 2011, as I was growing my young downtown Orlando ghost tour business, I decided to expand by also offering haunted pub tours. As the city's historic district is a virtual hotbed of paranormal activity, finding haunted drinking establishments was not a challenge. The real test would be gaining the collaborative cooperation of bar owners and management in venues that can be at times noisy, bustling, and well, under the influence of large amounts of alcohol, and those who have happily indulged. Planning, timing, and smooth execution would be just as important as the ghost stories or history of any of the selected locations.

Once I established what I thought was a workable first run tour of fun and interesting stops, I eagerly advertised the new offering, and solicited my drinking age guests.

While free media coverage and promotions are often welcome in business, I was dismayed, however, to find that my inaugural group would include "Kate", a local nightlife reviewer and some of her friends. I pleaded with her to give me a few weeks to work out the kinks that are common in a new venture before taking the tour, but she firmly resisted that suggestion. The tickets had already been purchased, and she would be there. And she would be taking notes on EVERYTHING.

The evening arrived for the first scheduled pub tour, and I had to battle away any anxiety over the details or the possible outcomes that haunted my sleep, and just take the plunge. So with another one of my guides, I prepared as well as I could for it. On time as promised, Kate appeared with her friends at the meeting place, and I could not help feeling a slight sense of renewed dread. Nevertheless, I cordially welcomed the group, reminding them that this was the very first pub tour, in the hope that she would be forgiving in the event that any of the million things that could go wrong actually did.

It should be noted that the guests were also excited about a new ghost app that had recently debuted, and many of them had downloaded it to their phones. This particular app was designed to mimic the function of an electronic piece of equipment called an Ovilus, which allows spirits to "speak" by selecting from a dictionary of words and names digitally stored in its memory. Still a skeptic of any device or program that is connected to the Internet, and primarily designed for entertainment purposes, I have seen the app deliver eerily appropriate during some investigations over the years since. At this time, however, I was mostly wary of the accuracy of this new craze. In the end I decided, whatever, as long as they had fun, generally enjoyed the evening, and delivered some positive feedback my way, it was not important.

Predictably, as the evening progressed and we traveled from one bar to another, we encountered issues more annoying than haunting, mostly involving the timing of drink service in busy locales. As I feared, this had not escaped the notice of Kate and her entourage, and with every hiccup revealed, it appeared to be duly noted. While each location had haunts and stories connected to it, and these were shared with the guests over drinks at every turn, nothing particularly paranormal is usually experienced in a hopping bar scene. Or at least that's what I thought.

While not paying much heed to what I deemed to be an odd coincidence, at least three times, in different places, Kate's friends and guests pointed out that the ghost app came up with her name and the number "12". Kate herself was puzzled by the repeated mention of her name and the number, but could not personally think of any connection, despite the effort.

When finally the tour came to an end, the strange occurrences appeared to be dismissed, and the foibles of the evening's pub crawl were instead addressed. I once again attempted to appeal to her and her guests' reasonableness, reminding them that this had been only the inaugural event, but was left with a slightly less than satisfactory feeling.

When the three and one-half out of five star review was published shortly after, I was disappointed, although not entirely surprised. While the piece was not stellar, it also was not particularly damaging to our tours, which continued to gain popularity. Still, I felt the need to reach out and discuss the experience with Kate, in the hopes that she might give another tour a chance.

Repeated calls and messages to her went unanswered, however, and I began to wonder what I may have done to offend her.

Finally, on my last attempt to contact Kate, her husband answered the phone. He delicately informed me that she would not be returning my calls at anytime, as she had recently passed away unexpectedly! After some stunned silence, he explained that she had gone quietly in her sleep, only in her mid-thirties, and was not considered to be unhealthy. It would not be until after that conversation, and my assistant at the time reading Kate's obituary, that an eerie connection would be made. Kate died exactly twelve days after the pub tour!

Whether this was some extreme freak coincidence, or an actual paranormal prophecy, I can't say for sure. But to this day I have yet to experience anything quite like it, and now have more questions than ever. I do want to end by offering wishes for Kate, that she be resting in sweet peace, and that all of her family and friends have found comfort.

K2 meters aka EMF detectors that we use during our investigations.

The Highland House

In every city across the country, if we searched, we could find countless homes that are legitimately haunted. Orlando is no exception, as I have mentioned earlier in some of my own personal experiences. It is of course, also not true that only the oldest houses or buildings harbor spirits from long past, or that they even have to die at that location to haunt there. Ghosts stay, return, or pass through places for their own reasons, many of which we may never understand. I would also like to point out that if I conducted a paranormal investigation in every single house or building to which I have been invited, I would barely have time for anything else!

Aside from our function as a ghost tour company for entertainment, my team and I are regularly asked to investigate paranormal activity in a variety of commercial buildings, to which we occasionally oblige. Much less often, under special circumstances, we also investigate private residences. The only purpose is to offer some answers to curious or frightened homeowners, and never to clear or confront dark entities. That we leave to the appropriate clergy!

It was by way of a repeat downtown AGA tour guest then that I found my way to the Highland House in October of 2017. The woman, a hairdresser, had convinced me to check out a suspected haunting in a local salon. With this done and a light level of spirit activity confirmed, she proceeded to pique my curiosity by mentioning the house of some friends, which she hinted had an interesting history and was slated to be torn down in the near future to make way for a new one. She thought it would be great if I could investigate it before then.

So there I was, early to arrive and parked on the street, staring up at the two-story mess of a house, while awaiting the arrival of the hairdresser and her friends. As I waited, two things became instantly obvious. First of all, situated among a street full of upscale, neatly tended homes, this nearly ninety-year-old house was in noticeable disrepair and exuded a state of abandonment, with its landscape nothing more than a tangle of overgrown weeds. Where once stood a proud family home, now a shabby shadow of its former self seemed to slink back from the curb. The second thing I noticed was an elderly woman peering at me from a second-floor corner window. After I squinted and briefly looked away, she was gone. But almost immediately I saw the same woman again, this time by the downstairs front door!

I blinked , and the old woman again had disappeared from view, just as the hairdresser drove up. She quickly jumped out of her car and began pulling Halloween decorations from the open trunk, while explaining that the house was completely vacant, and that the family who now owned it would be along shortly! This was something I had already suspected, but froze in place when I heard it said out loud. It turned out that the home had actually been abandoned for nearly a decade. In the meantime, the place was being used as a neighborhood haunted house attraction, the fake, fun kind that is, for the month of October.

The kicker was that the family believed that the house was genuinely haunted and wanted some answers, before they occupied the property. Now this was sounding more interesting by the minute!

After a brief wait, we were greeted by a slightly nervous looking family of four, consisting of a father, mother, young son and daughter. They appeared anxious for some information about their recent purchase, yet fearful about what they might actually learn. Our group now assembled, we embarked on a tour of the property, with my one request being that they not divulge any history or background information until I requested it. I would start by following my own intuition and perceptions.

Once inside, I determined that the first floor foyer and kitchen area felt relatively normal, while a living/sitting room off to the left was downright "peaceful and calm". This was despite the fact that the interior was garishly decorated for Halloween for a macabre and horrific effect, with fake blood spattered sheets and gauzy cobwebs, as well as a crib positioned in the middle of the sitting room as an apparent jumping out place for some ghoulish actor to scare the unsuspecting. We moved on to the sun porch facing the lake, out to the sad jumbled remains of a garden, and then down to the basement, a rare architectural feature in Florida. While "spooky" in that way that basements usually are, due to the fact that they are mostly dark, damp subterranean vaults, the space felt devoid of any unusual energy to me. In fact, none of the areas I had visited thus far were particularly notable.

We proceeded toward the stairs to the second floor. It was on the fourth step that all of the hairs on my body immediately stood on end. With my head now also throbbing, I heard my own voice announce to the others, "Somebody stands here." With that, we continued on up to the landing. A detoured climb up into the walkable attic from the pull-down stairs in the hallway yielded nothing out of the ordinary, only a dusty storage space. Back down on the second floor, I found myself in a front bedroom, facing the street. While peering out the window, I realized at once that this was the place where I had first seen the old woman gazing at me! But again, all was quiet. She wasn't there anymore, only the six of us. Likewise, the adjacent master bedroom felt just as empty.

It would be across the hall, in the room overlooking the remains of the garden and the lake beyond, that the purpose of my visit would be realized.

The bedroom, which was decorated in a striking green hue, was buzzing with energy! Drawn right away to the window, I felt inclined to proclaim, "She stands here." And then while glancing at the rest of the group, I added, "There's somebody here." Judging by their facial expressions, it was obvious that they could also feel the presence, especially the couple's daughter.

At that moment, a flashlight that I had placed in the window came on, as if to validate what everyone was sensing. There was a spirit in the room! I knew in that moment that it was the woman I had seen earlier in the window and at the front door. Now it was time to maybe get some answers.

Before continuing with our investigation, however, I finally requested the background history and any other pertinent information about the house from my awed companions.

The story that unfolded from the owners, along with some follow-up team research, was that of an original owner family of five. The couple and their two sons and one daughter would move on from the house at various different times and circumstances. After many years living together in the home, the father would pass on first, and his wife, nearly ten years later, after having moved away to live with family elsewhere in Florida.

With the children grown and mostly moved on, only one son would return and live in the home before it was finally left vacant, yet still furnished, almost a decade ago. It was this son who would leave it so tragically for the last time, having shot himself to death in the house. And it is he that the neighbors believed haunted it to the very day we stood inside.

As the story was related and the various family members mentioned, the flashlight began turning on and off persistently, and in a somewhat excited manner, as if in acknowledgement. The spirit would ultimately reveal that it was the mother, who had returned to the home she loved, to gaze upon the garden she once tended, and reunite with her troubled son. She also revealed that the green room had once been her beloved daughter's room, and that she identified affectionately with the young girl who would occupy the home in the near future.

When I addressed her by the name of the lady who had once owned the house, she verified that it was indeed her. Even more stunning, when I mentioned that I believed a man was also present in the house, the Rem Pod that I had placed down on the stairway abruptly and noisily went off, startling the whole group! Although the man's name could not be identified, when we referenced the woman's son, the Rem Pod again sounded. Interestingly, it was also revealed that the man had taken his life down in the sitting room, which felt exceedingly calm. Perhaps his troubled soul was now actually at peace.

It was now time to explain to the vigilant spirit that the house was set to be demolished, and that a new home for the new family was to be built in its place. She promptly turned on the flashlight to indicate that she understood. The stunned new owners then expressed to her that she was welcome to stay and watch over the property for as long as she wished.

 Again the light came on. We reluctantly concluded the fascinating ghostly interaction by reciting a blessing for all.

While the old house no longer exists, the neighbors reported that the old woman could still be seen gazing out of the windows up until the demolition. Now I am waiting to hear whether she continues to frequent the new home, where she had been invited to stay by her new friends, and adopted family. I will keep you posted!

The Place that "Eddie" Built

In 1884, the biggest fire in Orlando history virtually wiped out a portion of the business district in the young, but growing downtown. Originating at Delaney's Grocery Store on the corner of Pine Street and Magnolia Avenue, the conflagration swept through many of the wooden buildings that lined the dusty streets. Amazingly, nobody was killed or seriously injured, but the fledgling city was caught off guard, with no organized fire department to stanch the destruction of the ravaging inferno.

That event served to usher in a new direction for Orlando, which now featured a properly equipped fire department, and a building code that required more resistant brick and mortar construction. One of the prominent local businessmen, Edward Kuhl, promptly jumped in on the effort, and together with James Delaney, he helped to erect the new "Phoenix" building on top of the ashes of the latter's demolished grocery store. Further inspired by the reconstruction efforts, in 1886, Kuhl also built himself a three-story brick structure, directly across from the Phoenix. In addition to the ornately sophisticated English Club and Cosmopolitan Club, established by an Englishman named Gordon Rogers on the opposite corner, the intersection of Pine and Magnolia was fully transformed.

A young German immigrant, who made his way to Orlando in 1873 from Mississippi, following a stint as a calvaryman in the Civil War, Edward Kuhl quickly became a distinguished local business leader. In 1886, he helped found the Orlando Board of Trade, the precursor to the Chamber of Commerce, and served as its first president. His various businesses included a candy store located on Church Street. Most importantly, he was what we would now call "a mover and a shaker", as he settled into his new building at 68 East Pine Street. Unfortunately, he would not have long to enjoy his burgeoning success.

On May 25, 1888, Edward Kuhl climbed the flight of stairs from the second floor to his third floor office one last time. Halfway up, somewhere in the middle, he collapsed and died suddenly, the victim of a massive heart attack at just forty-five years of age.

But as many know, those who have either owned or worked there in the years since, he may have never really left the building!

As a parade of businesses came and went over time, the occupants often noted strange occurrences. This is particularly true of the various drinking establishments that have taken up there, to include the current ones. Glasses would mysteriously slide off the bar unassisted and shatter on the floor, while liquor bottles would disappear and reappear in the time it takes a lone bartender to turn his or her back. Even a light bulb from high above one bar would inexplicably go missing, only to turn up in the oddest of places, such as the ice bin or an employee's handbag. The manager had even marked the bulb with an X to track its strange movements. One day, while immediately opening a sealed box of supplies that had been delivered, he discovered the bulb inside, complete with the X in his own handwriting!

On yet another occasion, the staff unpacked a delivery and stocked the bar before leaving for the rest of the night. Upon returning the next day, they found all of the empty boxes had been stacked up against the bar door from the inside!

It would be a previous lounge owners' young son who inadvertently provided a name to the merry prankster. The pre-school aged boy often accompanied his parents to the building during the day when they worked at various business chores. As they went about their duties, he would wander off and play on the different floors. After some time he began to talk about a new friend, whom he called "Eddie". The puzzled parents could not recall a youngster by that name among his regular playmates, nor could they locate him when they searched his class list, or any other groups with which he interacted. They reluctantly concluded that Eddie was an invisible friend, the kind that some children invent when they are lonely.

The child was insistent, however, that Eddie was real and not invisible, at least to him, and was most definitely not a little boy. He was the fun, kindly man whom the lad played with regularly, but only at his parents' building. The Kuhl Building, that Edward Kuhl built, and where he worked hard and died tragically. Of course, Eddie!

While secondhand stories inspire our AGA tours and investigations, it is our team's own personal experiences that really bring validation and substance to our narrative, as with all of the stories herein. And it is in the Kuhl Building where we have seen the prankster side of Eddie firsthand. Especially for one guide and her trainee, who accompanied her on a tour one evening in 2016.

The guide led a group of guests up to the second floor and into the dark enclosed area through the door from the small bar, where we at one time could take our tours to quietly investigate.

As so frequently happened, some of the guests were instantly drawn to the closed door that hid the stairway leading to the third floor. There was no mistaking the heavy feeling that emanated from that area, and although none of them yet knew the reason, they were intrigued. After the guests had a chance to investigate for a few minutes, and once they were seated, the guide related the history and stories about the building, especially regarding Eddie the prankster.

While each and every tour is completely different, and the spirits themselves determine whether or not the group will experience any paranormal activity in a haunted location, Eddie did not disappoint. At the mention of his name, a flashlight in the room came on and turned off by itself, and the Rem Pod by the stairway door even blipped at one point. Although no new information was learned as the guides and guests asked questions, Edward Kuhl had definitely made his presence known to the stunned visitors.

With the visit there over, the guide and her assistant performed the customary duty of picking up the equipment used and returning it to the shouldered gear bag, while accounting for each piece in the process, to include the $60 K2 meters provided and carried by guests. Confident that all had been secured and the area was left as they had found it, they departed for their next and final investigation spot. It would be at this time that they noticed that one of the extra meters was missing, one that had not been used or removed from the bag that evening. With all of the numbered K2 meters properly collected from the guests, a quick count and then several recounts by both guides, confirmed that there were only nine meters when there should be ten. All compartments of the bag were inspected to no avail.

They would have to retrace their steps and return to the last place that they saw all ten.

Personally and financially responsible for the equipment they carry on each tour, the panicked guides hurried back to the Kuhl Building. Up in the second floor room where the tour had taken place, they searched every inch, from couches to the bar area where Eddie liked to snatch the light bulb. No meter. Frustrated, they sat down to consider their options, especially how they would tell me, "the boss", about the careless loss. It was as they talked that they absentmindedly unzipped the gear bag once again, even though they knew what they would find. Looking in one last time, the shock of what they saw almost knocked them both over. There were ten meters! Though it seemed impossible, there they were all neatly lined up in two rows of five, the missing one now among them! There was no explanation of how it reappeared, but there were suspicions. Eddie strikes again!

So how do we know it was him? Because he told us! During later tours to the building when the guides would retell the story and then ask Edward Kuhl whether he was the culprit, the flashlight would flicker on, almost as if he were laughing! And he always gets the last laugh at his place.

Before the second floor bar area was opened up and remodeled in recent years, and the dark, quiet area we used was available for some quality communication with the spirits, we learned a lot about Eddie from the man himself. This included that he likes to be called Eddie, or even Edward sometimes, but never Mr. Kuhl. He confirmed his life history, even telling us that he was a young man when he arrived in the U.S. Most importantly, he claimed that he had had a good life, and that he was happy still, while interacting with the living, especially through harmless, good humored pranks.

On one particular tour we learned something else about Eddie.

During this session with a small group of young people in their twenties, he was especially responsive. The flashlight on the bar in the room consistently turned on and off intelligently, and he seemed to have an affinity for the female guide that evening, while eager for the group to get to know him. At one point, as they all were in the middle of a "conversation", the door from the adjacent bar area opened and two somewhat intoxicated young ladies stumbled in, in search of the nearby restroom. Instantly, the flashlight on the bar turned off. When the slurry women inquired as to what everyone was doing there in the dark, the answer was that they were "just sitting here awhile." Once the ladies had completed their restroom mission, they stumbled back past the group and out the way they had come. No sooner had the door shut behind them, the flashlight popped back on brighter than ever. Eddie was still there, ready and waiting to continue the conversation. But only with the sober people!

So now we know. When you come to play at Eddie's place, enjoy yourself, but drink responsibly, or you just might become the unsuspecting victim of an inveterate prankster!

Extended Stay at the Old Orlando Hotel

As the sun sets west of downtown Orlando, blasts of live entertainment, or the chatter and cheers of sporting events flashing on multiple TV screens, drift up and over the mezzanine from the first floor bar below. Meanwhile, the hallways and rooms up on the third floor sink into dark shadows. Dating back to 1924, the building at the corner of Church Street and Garland Avenue originally served as Slemons Department Store, and later the renowned Rosie O'Grady's Good Time Emporium, while presently home to Harry Buffalo restaurant and bar. The very top story, however, is where the Orlando Hotel once thrived, and maybe today, where history lives on. Although its small, traditionally efficient rooms are now cluttered with restaurant equipment and other cast-off storage items, the hotel is still very much "occupied".

For the past six years or so it is also currently the base for American Ghost Adventures; and while not otherwise accessible to the general public, it is usually the final stop for our ghost tours. It's because it may be the final stop for some "others", however, that makes it a special place to me and my guides. And it has subsequently offered up a host of paranormal experiences for us, and for many of our guests as well.

Just as with any commercial building and property that enjoys a long history, and that has been frequented by countless people and their respective energies, most of the spirit activity cannot be attributed to any particular, identifiable figures. Nevertheless, we are very fortunate to have the acquaintance of several resident ghosts who do wish to frequently interact with the living. That said, anyone who has worked in the building, be it tour guide or restaurant employee, they will tell you that the third floor's eerie atmosphere, whether day or night, can be quite unsettling. Doors that open and close on their own, cold spots, disembodied footsteps, shadow figures and moving objects are just a few of the reasons why the downstairs staff make only quick trips to the storage areas above, especially after dark!

Our mission, aside from entertaining willing guests in spooky, haunted places, is to attempt to communicate with those who are haunting. If that all happens at the same time, all the better. Thankfully, the more time we spend with these spirits, the more likely they are to oblige us. Being respectful of their stories and personalities, and showing our appreciation for their cooperation also goes a long way. After awhile some of them come to seem like friends, and even family, who try to help us as we do them. Although in some cases, their "help" might be just a little alarming.

So it was with one of our tour guides, an aspiring actor, who despite his job title which includes "ghost ambassador" and "paranormal investigator", was especially easy to spook.

The young man led his tour group upstairs, and down the pitch black halls into what we call "the big room", where a somewhat surly spirit named Kevin is known to occupy a particular space when he is present. It should be stated, that he is not happy to have visitors intrude on this space, and he has made his feelings known. Guests who violate Kevin's territory have been touched, or made to feel deeply uncomfortable. Although not dangerous, or malevolent in any way, it is best not to irritate or disrespect somebody who can see you, but you can't see them!

After the guests had an opportunity to investigate with the equipment, the guide related stories about Kevin and other spirits encountered in the building.

Noting that there did not appear to be any real activity on that evening, as is sometimes the case, he prepared to move the group on to a final stop down the hall. Now when we talk about activity, we mean that the guests' meters were not spiking, nor were any of the flashlights placed around the room coming on. Additionally, the cylinder-shaped Rem Pod, with its antenna extended and its battery switched on, remained silent in its place flat on the floor in front of Kevin's spot.

As he proceeded to pick up the various pieces of equipment, the guide reminded the guests that while activity has happened there, it is never guaranteed, and is generally beyond our control as tour guides. It was at this very moment that the Rem Pod turned onto its side and rolled straight across the floor untouched, only stopping when it reached the startled guide's feet! He promptly inquired of the stunned guests, all of whom had witnessed the incident, whether anyone had touched the device.

With no person in the room even in close proximity to it at the time, it was already clear that nobody had, or at least, nobody who was living. The shaken guide gave up all pretense of professional calm and quickly hustled his guests from the room. It is an understatement to say that it was a very dramatic end to one tour! It would be during later tours led by other guides that Kevin would own up to being the rolling Rem Pod perpetrator, turning on a flashlight in response, in front of yet more groups of astounded guests. Several sensitive guests, as well as psychics, have consistently described Kevin as a grouchy older man, with scraggly longish hair, wearing overalls, who apparently died in the building many years ago.

One other former guide who may or may not have experienced Kevin, but definitely experienced "something", was caught up in the ritual post-tour closing up on the third floor that we all must do.

A seasoned, but self-described skeptical "paranormal investigator", he went about his business, beginning in the big room. With the summer season in its full drop-dead humid mode, the air conditioner window unit is a must-have for all tours at that time. It also must be turned off at the end of the tours, so the guide set about doing so. With his back to the room, he squinted in the murky darkness for the power button. Suddenly, he felt a large, strong hand clamp down and grip one of his shoulders. Believing he was the only person present on the third floor, he fearfully spun around to confront whoever had grabbed him, only to find the yawning, dark and empty room staring back at him! Known for his somewhat cocky, dry wit, and otherwise stoic nature, he would reluctantly later admit that he had never walked out so fast from anywhere before in his entire life, while shaking uncontrollably. What's more, as per company post-tour requirements, he was on the phone with me checking out at the time he was touched. I actually heard him scream like a little girl, and drop the phone!

Where Kevin's Rem Pod prank and the shoulder grab could be interpreted as either mischievous or intimidating, depending on whom you ask, other experiences at the old hotel could be described as maybe even more hair-raising. This would be the case for another longtime guide, who was also closing down upstairs by himself following a tour. Once again, it should be mentioned that being alone on the third floor at night can rate high on the spooky spectrum. And it is especially so when experiencing the sounds of footsteps and seeing the almost ever present darting shadows as we all navigate the end of the night procedures. Yet nothing prepared this experienced guide for what would happen to him.

The gentleman was in the process of neatening and arranging the gear bag and equipment in the area near the exit stairs, where we kept our file cabinet at the time.

The reason for this arrangement was due to the fact that back then, the only source of light was this playtime. He and the other spirits have even wished guests a happy birthday by flickering flashlights along with the song as we sing. Aaron has indicated that he loves dogs, and in particular Rin Tin Tin, who was a movie star dog of the 1920's, and later of 50's television. We have brought in Rin Tin Tin comics and a book just for him, which he signaled he likes very much. Whether it's Aaron, or someone else, we have had balls roll across the floor on their own, and even a toy fire engine flash on by itself several times, in front of amazed guests.

Once, prior to a tour, the lone guide announced to the empty room that she would be bringing some guests to play later, and asked if that would be okay with "everyone". As she finished her setup in the Merch Room, she heard the sound of something hitting the floor in the adjacent Research Room. She went to investigate, and there in the middle of the floor was a bean bag bunny that had moments before been sitting at the back of the shelf with the other toys! During the subsequent tour, to the delight of the guests, Aaron turned on the flashlight to answer that it was he who had tossed the bunny, to let the guide know he was ready to play!

To this day, our team and our guests still enjoy visits with Aaron, as well as with many other mostly nameless spirits. Our surveillance cameras have caught after hours moving orbs around the toys, and even following our guests and spiking their meters during tours. One camera actually caught a door flying open in the middle of the night when nobody was in the building! It is safe to say that even though it is no longer a hotel, the rooms are anything but vacant!

A Majestic Hotel

Once upon a time, before magical mice and wizards staked their empires in Central Florida, the area surrounding The City Beautiful was a patchwork of large and small homesteads, expansive cattle ranches and farms, and prosperous orange groves. Savvy land buys that started in the 1950's and 60's would ultimately alter the landscape, and give way to a sprawling tourist mecca, that today draws millions of vacation hungry travelers from every corner of the world. To feed the ever growing demand for rooms, hotels, resorts, and timeshare developments of every style and price point have sprouted up across the region. And as with most hotels located anywhere, these destinations are now haunted by many of the souls and energies who have relaxed, or sadly expired, inside their walls.

It is here among the attractions, eateries and retail strip centers that make up the bustling tourist corridor that one large timeshare – turned- hotel landed on our ghost radar.

Situated on a parcel of former cow pasture, this five-story resort building is only several decades old. At first glance, its odd layout and eerie, quiet hallways just seem to be a bit "off". But they belie the true buzz of ghostly Hrods on the building may have anything to do with the atmosphere, nobody can tell. Either way, through personal experience, and with guests as witnesses, I can say that the place is undeniably haunted!

Stories that have been passed along by management and staff include the periodic apparition of a dusty cowboy, who appears to be passing through before simply vanishing. Whether he's on an eternal mission to keep track of a long ago herd, or just the residual energy of a vigilant wrangler, it's hard to tell. Everyone who has witnessed him agrees, however, that he seems unaware that he is on a hotel property, or to notice others around him as he goes about his ghostly ranching business.

Other strange phenomena involve the automatic doors that lead out to the pool area. They have been observed to repeatedly open and close as if someone, or something, were running in and out, but with nobody actually in the vicinity. Maintenance examinations could find nothing wrong with the doors, or any other reasonable explanation for the malfunctions. The exasperated manager finally asked me what I thought about these disquieting occurrences. Sensing the presence of playful child spirits, who may be fascinated by these modern conveniences and the power to trigger them, I suggested that he simply ask them, "Please stop, and go play somewhere else now," whenever the doors began to act up on their own. The staff subsequently took my advice, and each time they addressed the spirits, the doors mysteriously and abruptly stopped! Sometimes all you need to do is ask nicely.

My suggestion of the existence of ghost children at the hotel was not a novel thought by any means. Guests have reported (or complained about, as the case may be) hearing children laughing and playing in the hallways in the dead of night. When the sleepy and thoroughly irritated patrons storm out to confront the unruly, poorly parented imps, there is not a soul in sight. Any children who may actually be present in the hotel are fast asleep with their families behind locked doors. Sometimes, however, there is not even one child on the property at all! As to the questions of who are these ghost children and why are they there, the answers are beyond anybody's guess.

Cowboys and children are not the only haunts to catch the attention of anyone who frequents this resort. In a fifth floor window overlooking the pool area, the figure of a man has been spotted peering out. Immediate physical examinations of that upper floor area have frequently found no living person, but instead, the searchers are met with a persistent heavy and uncomfortable feeling. It should be noted that due to a fire, this floor is closed off to guests, and functions as a storage area for old, unused furniture, televisions and signage. For obvious reasons, the staff also avoids going up there at all costs!

A description of the paranormal activity would not be complete without mentioning the continued devotion of a certain former employee. "David" was always on time for his shift behind the Front Desk, and no employer could ever ask for a more dependable worker. So on the day he failed to show up for work as scheduled, the rest of the staff was immediately concerned. When he was once again no-show on the following day, concern turned into alarm. After all attempts to reach David were unsuccessful, it was decided that a welfare check at his apartment was necessary. Sadly, it was there that he was discovered, dead in his chair from a massive heart attack.

For an employee as conscientious as David, however, absence from a job and a place that he had enjoyed was out of the question. Consequently, he is still seen and felt at the hotel to this day. A man fitting his description has been observed in the kitchenette area, and it is here that our team met him and confirmed his continued presence. When we set up a flashlight in this area and asked for any spirits who wanted to communicate to please turn it on, it came on brightly. Through a subsequent question and response session, David let us know that it was indeed him, and that he was fine. When we offered to bring him his favorite fast food, which he ate every day on the job, he turned the light on in agreement. Of course, when we make promises, we always follow through, and we brought David his favorite meal.

While we were able to identify one of the resident spirits by name, it is not so clear who else may be frequenting the hotel.

During our special tours and investigations over the years, we were able to observe knocking sounds in the first floor conference rooms that could not be explained. The only thing we were able to establish was that they would occur around 9:00 p.m., with no known origin that we or the staff could find. Additionally, our tour guests reported experiencing heavy feelings in certain areas, and once again, flashlights would turn on to alert as to various presences as we investigated both the first and fifth floors.

During one tour, I was determined that we would find a way to play with the spirits so that they would enjoy interacting with us. Armed with a child's ball, as well as two plastic cups and a plastic Easter egg, we prepared to entice them. I first asked one guest, a self-admitted believer in ghosts, to put the egg under one of the cups while everyone else in the room looked away. We then set a flashlight by each of the two cups and asked the spirits if they could tell us which of the cups concealed the egg.

After several moments, one of the flashlights came on. I promptly went over and lifted the cup next to it. There was the egg! A repeat of the game using another guest again revealed the hidden egg.

One very vocal, avowed skeptic in the group declared himself to be unimpressed, while convinced that it was more of a rigged set up rather than a paranormal event. We love our skeptics, and I happily invited him to set up the next round himself, to include both flashlights, the cups and the egg. He smugly did so and returned to his seat on one side of the room. When asked if the spirits could now find the egg, a slightly longer period of time slipped by with no response. Then suddenly, a flashlight came on, piercing the dark room. But this one was not next to either one of the cups. Instead, it was one of the other flashlights that had been placed around the room earlier, and this one was located right next to where the skeptic was seated.

The stunned gentleman leapt to his feet and quickly revealed that, to prove his point, he had slipped the egg into his pocket rather than leaving it under one of the cups! Now a little less cocky, he promptly tried to hand off the egg to his startled girlfriend next to him, who was having none of it as she bolted away. It just goes to show, you can fool some of the people some of the time, but you can never really fool the spirits! Thanks for playing, sir!

I would like to make one final note about this quite active property. Aside from the hauntings that occur within, another natural phenomenon can be found outside in the grassy area adjacent to the building. Called a "fairy circle" or "fairy ring", it is a group of mushrooms growing in a perfect circle, which is often seen during certain times of the year. Just one more mystery for a place that harbors so many!

A (Not So) Final Resting Place

Just as a city must make room for its growing population of the living, so too must it find plenty of resting space for the dead.

So it was for Orlando in the late nineteenth century. By 1880, it was obvious that the region's small church graveyards and the many scattered family plots were not practical in accommodating the interment needs of its ever increasing number of residents. Thus, a search for a larger, more central property was undertaken by several of the city's prominent leaders, and prosperous investors. Twenty-six acres were subsequently purchased southeast of downtown, and the Orlando Cemetery became the new burial ground.

Purchased by the city in later years and renamed Greenwood Cemetery, it now encompasses one-hundred acres, nestled in the heart of quiet, tree-lined neighborhoods. With a Who's Who of eminent and ordinary Orlandoans in attendance, the gravestones, crypts and markers are an historical testament to the ends of sad stories, as well as to the many lives well-lived. Military veterans and war heroes, martyrs and the tragically unfortunate, revered icons and civic leaders, the very young and the blessedly old, the workadays and the wealthy, the unheralded and the colorfully eccentric, all share one common distinction: Orlando citizens worthy of burial inside the gates of Greenwood.

As with most cemeteries, Greenwood beckons the curious who wish to communicate with any of the spirits who may be restless and seeking interaction with the living. That, of course, includes us. Being a paranormal investigative tour group, we are always eager to explore with our guests, albeit after hours only when permitted, and in a manner respectful to the deceased and their loved ones. Once again, while we enjoy the fascinating history and the oft told stories, it is our own personal experiences in the cemetery that we really endeavor to pass on to others.

Anyone is free to wander the looping roads and the rows of tranquil gravesites during the daytime when the gates are open.

But after hours, only those invited and supervised by city staff may walk the grounds without fear of trespass. We have been fortunate to have had just such a relationship with the City of Orlando, and have been allowed to lead tour groups there several times a year, most years, for over a decade. It is during these visits, and some of the pre-tour daytime excursions, that we have experienced some extraordinary events. On several of these occasions, we learned that the spirits can be very helpful!

In my early years as a co-owner of the company that preceded AGA, I found myself exploring the cemetery with my then partner. On one particular day, we were attempting to locate a certain gravesite, but being still unfamiliar with the layout, we were having no luck. As we bumbled about the landscape for what seemed like forever, our meters and a digital recorder in hand, I suddenly felt compelled to suggest that we make a turn to the right.

Almost immediately we arrived at the elusive grave. What we did not yet realize, however, was that we may have received some otherworldly assistance. When playing back the recording we had made during our search, we heard something most interesting. Just after we questioned out loud which direction we should go, and seconds before I suggested turning right, a raspy voice states, "Right"! Neither of us had heard the voice with our own ears in real time, but there it was, a crystal clear EVP (Electronic Voice Phenomenon)! What's more, we had acted on it!

On another day visit years later, I once again attempted to locate a specific grave. It was that of a spirit with whom I had connected on a downtown tour, at the place where he had tragically died in a fire nearly fifty years before. With both of us being firefighters, we had seemingly bonded and he extended a warning of "danger" to me, apparently in reference to my job.

Now I wanted to find his gravesite and pay my respects. Carrying an Ovilus , just as I had on the previously mentioned tour, I weaved about, certain that I was somewhere near the correct location. Having no success, I began to feel frustrated, and somewhat drained by the relentless humidity. Suddenly the Ovilus began to "talk" to me. A string of prompts set me walking again, which appropriately included "13", "observe", "highway", "east", "rewind", "foliage" and "down". As I obediently followed along, in a matter of minutes, I was standing in Section 13, looking down at his tombstone! Without the helpful directions, I might still be wandering!

While visiting on yet another occasion, I encountered a spirit who wanted to redirect me to his own grave as I was attempting to speak to somebody else, with whom we had communicated in the past. I made my way over to July Perry's grave, just past the office, on the left, in what was once the segregated section for the African-American citizens of Orlando. The now venerated Mr. Perry is a stark figure from the area's more sinister past history. A victim of horrendous torture and a lynching on Election Day in November, 1920, he had originally been dumped into an unmarked grave, all for having registered black voters. With a new gravestone and more widespread honor and acknowledgement of his life and ultimate sacrifice, we never come to Greenwood without visiting him and leaving flowers.

Occasionally, he will respond back to us, turning on a flashlight or setting off other devices as we relate his story. On this day, however, there was no response from Mr. Perry. As I wished him peace and prepared to leave, the Ovilus I had with me started to speak. But it clearly was not from July Perry. The prompts were giving me directions, along with the letter "I". Extremely curious to see where this was leading me, I followed along.

Within a minute, I had located the grave of a gentleman by the name of Isaac, just a short distance from the Perry grave! He then confirmed that it was he who had summoned me by turning on a flashlight! Since this initial encounter, we have done some research on him as well, and to this day, he also occasionally communicates with us when we visit with our tours. It just goes to show, that sometimes the spirits just want to be acknowledged.

For many people, the old saying, "seeing is believing" describes the ultimate paranormal experience. Whether it is a full bodied apparition, a shadow, a moving object, or some other inexplicable visual phenomenon, it is the stuff that makes even skeptics take note. Of course, not everybody agrees that seeing something is such a great experience. Sometimes it is more the stuff of nightmares.

Quite a few years back, when my youngest son was just a little boy, he accompanied me on one of my day visits to the cemetery.

As I have previously mentioned before, he is somewhat sensitive to spirits, but past experiences have been relatively benign. As I conducted my business with the office staff, he happily played with his toy car outside on the pavement. Suddenly, he leapt to his feet and screamed, "Monster!" His brown eyes were wide with terror as he stared beyond at the section adjacent to the ash gate, near the cemetery entrance. I rushed to him, scanning the area at which he continued to stare in horror, but could see nothing, living or otherwise to explain the outburst. When I asked him to describe exactly what he saw, he once again shrieked, "Monster!" Inconsolable, he demanded that we leave at once. While I would never know what he really saw, I knew my son well enough to believe him when he claimed to see something that so completely frightened him, even in the bright light of day.

Nighttime brings a whole other dimension to Greenwood Cemetery.

On most nights, except for the clear, moonlit ones, the darkness shrouds the area so completely, that even those familiar with its layout can easily become turned around and lost. It also makes the capture of apparitions and visual anomalies by both the naked eye and camera more startling.

Shadow figures have been witnessed by numerous visitors, especially around the impressive crypt of the disgruntled Fred Weeks. Mr. Weeks has reportedly been seen pacing in front of the structure he built with his own hands, still fuming over having been swindled in an Orlando land deal more than one hundred years ago. Despite settling with the offenders and subsequently agreeing to never reveal the men's prominent names, which he had originally carved on to the crypt door, Fred can't seem to rest. During our tours he has frequently turned on flashlights and set off Rem Pods by his tomb when asked about the long ago incident, perhaps in hopes that somebody will at least guess the names and end his eternal seething. Some of our guests have even captured interesting photos around the crypt, with some showing strange moving light anomalies shooting into the trees above, where no light source exists.

If experiencing just one apparition can be described as jaw dropping, imagine being able to see an entire group of apparitions! While leading a tour in the early years of visiting the cemetery, I brought my group to the military section, specifically near the Union and Confederate graves. As we paused to talk about the location, we all became aware of a shadowy group just down the way from us, that appeared to be marching and carrying lanterns. Bewildered, I called the other guide who was elsewhere in the cemetery with another group, and asked him as to their location.

He confirmed that he was on the opposite side, out of view from us, while also indicating that there were no other groups in there that night, and that the gates were locked. In stunned silence we all watched as the shadow figures disappeared into the darkness. What's more, I would later learn that some of the guests had been audio recording during the tour in an effort to catch EVP's. They had picked up the sound of marching boots on the ground right at that moment!

While we often do not see apparitions or shadow figures, our guests who take a lot of photos on our tours frequently capture strange anomalies among the gravestones. Fortunately for us, they are often eager to share them. Such was the case on a tour in the fall of 2019. One woman, who according to her husband, takes many interesting photos wherever she goes, continuously clicked away with her phone as the guide led the group around the various burial sections. At some points, she would step away from the group and arbitrarily aim off into various directions, taking random shots.

Near the end of the tour, as the guide was finishing stories atop the highest hill in the cemetery, the woman excitedly rushed forward. She had been reviewing the many recorded images on her phone and came across one that she found to be quite exceptional. In the photo, the flash appeared to illuminate a large gravestone, which could not be read. But it was what was behind the stone that was incredible. Standing there in the shot were three figures. Although the images were somewhat blurred and no facial features were recognizable, they were clearly that of a man and a woman holding the hands of a young girl between them. They appeared to be dressed in 1950's attire, with one in a bright red dress and the man in a white shirt and tie. Because we always look to explain or debunk an incident first, we all quickly noted that none of the guests in any of the four tour groups that night were dressed similarly, and there were no children at all on the tour!

Unfortunately as the stone could not be read, and the woman had no idea where she had taken the random shot over the two-hour tour, we have no idea who these people could be. Although we may never know the identities of the family, or their story, one thing is for certain: They were there, and they were together!

Finally, it's worth noting that some paranormal experiences involve other senses besides seeing and hearing. Sometimes it is tactile, involving touch, or even some extrasensory perception. Maybe it can be a combination of all of these. This was brought home to me on at least two exceptional occasions, during which a bonafide psychic was along to act as "interpreter". The first time, I was doing a daytime walkthrough of the cemetery with the psychic , when I suddenly felt drawn to the backside of one of the oldest sections, near the perimeter fence. As we approached the area, I kept feeling the sensation of something rushing past my bare legs, although there was no breeze that day, and nothing visibly near my skin. With the intensity increasing around my legs, I desperately searched for the source. The psychic smiled at my puzzlement and informed me that it was "the children" playing a game of tag with me. When asked who these children were, she promptly pointed in the direction of three very old and very faded identical headstones. It seems the apparent siblings were game to play with anyone was willing, or able! So if you are there and you feel a rush where there is no breeze, perhaps it is your turn to be "it"!

Another notable experience that was mediated by a psychic involved one of my longtime guides, while we were once again on our pre-tour reconnaissance walk. Although we do not as a practice dress in costume for tours, except maybe for special Halloween events, on this occasion he was wearing a cloak for dramatic effect.

In the area of some of the military graves on one side, and a childrens' section on the other, he was overcome by the sudden need to go and sit by a roadside bench there. With nothing physically wrong, he admitted that he had been testing his own intuitiveness and sensitivity, and felt compelled to sit on that bench. The psychic encouraged him to do so, stating that there was actually a little girl sitting there who wished to talk to him, while also wondering why he was dressed the way he was. The guide sat down and quickly became immersed in a conversation with the girl, seemingly no longer aware of his surroundings, or our presence. The girl warmly told him not to be afraid of his ability and to feel comfortable exploring his sensitivity! To this day, that remains one of the most unique and special experiences either I, or my guides, have had in the cemetery.

There are many fascinating stories about the people in repose at Greenwood, including some after death. In that vein in would be fitting to mention the grave of Ada Gopher, a "Seminole Indian" woman, as noted on her marker, who died in the mid twentieth century. Whether it is by coincidence, or by some other worldly means, a gopher tortoise has chosen to make its burrow beneath only her grave marker, and no others. Wisely, the cemetery staff reconsidered their inclination to fill in the hole that they had initially deemed a hazard. It is especially wise though, due to the fact that gopher tortoises are a protected species in Florida, and filling the hole would have surely trapped and suffocated the innocent reptile. But it may be even wiser to avoid the possible bad karma that might come from doing so!

We continue to bring interested and respectful visitors to Greenwood Cemetery, and appreciate the opportunity to learn about the residents there who have lived and gone before us. Of course, we are also grateful for any positive interactions they may choose to have with us. Most of all, we wish them peace.

The White Bench at Greenwood Cemetery

Ting and the AGA team continue to relay messages from those that have past by offering public investigations and tours. If you enjoyed the book, you can book your own ghost adventure at www.americanghostadventures.com. You can also find them on social media:

Facebook: American Ghost Adventures

Twitter: AmericanGhostCrew @ AGACrew

Instagram: Americanghostcrew

You Tube: American Ghost Adventures
https://www.youtube.com/channel/UCSr6TzU
MpiT7GiHYOhce4sg?view_as=subscriber